P9-DFQ-286

Marc Platt
Universal Pictures
The Araca Group   Jon B. Platt
and
David Stone
present

Kerry Ellis   Dianne Pilkington

WICKED

Music and Lyrics   Book
Stephen Schwartz   Winnie Holzman

Based on the novel by
Gregory Maguire

Also Starring

Oliver Tompsett

Caroline Keiff   Jeremy Legat   Andy Mace

Cindy Belliot   Matthew Boulton   Sabrina Carter   Nadine Cox   Matthew Croke
Aileen Donohoe   Sarah Earnshaw   A.C. Garcia   Ashleigh Gray   Kady-Jo Jackson
Keeley Jane Jackson   Alex Jessop   Aimee Lewis   Pippa Lloyd   Mitchell Mahony
Rachel Muldoon   Adam Murray   Sean Parkins   Jake Samuels   David Stoller
Liam Tamne   Chloe Taylor   Lindsay Taylor   Emily Tierney
Hannah Toy   George Ure   Tim Walton   Gary Wood

and

Harriet Thorpe   Desmond Barrit

Settings   Costumes   Lighting   Sound
Eugene Lee   Susan Hilferty   Kenneth Posner   Tony Meola

Projections   Wigs & Hair   Casting
Elaine J. McCarthy   Tom Watson   Pippa Ailion

UK Music Supervisor   Music Arrangements   Dance Arrangements
Joel Fram   Alex Lacamoire & Stephen Oremus   James Lynn Abbot

US Associate Director   Associate Choreographer   Associate Set Designer   UK Associate Director
Lisa Leguillou   Mark Myars   Edward Pierce   Petra Siniawski

Production Manager   General Management
Richard Bullimore   Act Productions - Nick Salmon & Nia Janis

US Management   UK Executive Producer
321 Theatrical Management   Michael McCabe

Orchestrations
William David Brohn

Music Supervisor
Stephen Oremus

Musical Staging by
Wayne Cilento

Directed by
Joe Mantello

Author Gregory Maguire wrote his novel *Wicked: The Life and Times of the Wicked Witch of the West* whilst living in London in 1990: The year that Iraqi troops invaded Kuwait, sparking the Persian Gulf War; Nelson Mandela was released from prison after over 27 years; East and West Germany were reunited and Margaret Thatcher resigned as Prime Minister. Here Gregory talks about some of his inspirations for the best-selling novel.

The affection we hold for the magical worlds of Narnia and Middle-earth, of Wonderland and Oz, is rooted in the lure of the weird - what Tolkien called "arresting strangeness." That subtle attraction to the strange is related to the appetite that tempts us, eventually, to nibble at olives soaked in gin when once we would only have accepted biscuits trailed through tepid milk.

In a novel by P.D. James, English philosopher Roger Scruton is quoted as saying "The consolation of the imaginary is not imaginary consolation." Such a consolation is partly curiosity, perhaps tinged with prurience, about the peculiar and the arcane. Another aspect of the consolation derives from the contrast between the heavyweight problems of our own lives and times and the relief that turning our attentions elsewhere affords. The imaginary (in this instance, literary fantasy) can at best be more than a distraction, if never quite a corrective.

Two cases in point. Tolkien's Middle-earth reinvigorated readers' interest in older narrative conceits of the hero in battle just as Europe was tumbling toward its mid-century paroxysms of genocide and war. ("The world is all grown strange... How shall a man judge what to do in such times?") Lewis Carroll, three quarters of a century earlier, had gently mocked Victorian certainties and niceties by portraying Wonderland as an anarchic dreamscape. For Lewis Carroll's readers, the very concepts of before and after would become muddled. ("Jam tomorrow and jam yesterday, but never jam today.") For his readers, with the almost contemporaneous appearance of Darwin's *The Voyage of the Beagle,* long-held notions about before and after would be turned upside-out and inside-down.

The Wonderful Wizard of Oz - that is, the original children's novel written by American writer L. Frank Baum, and published in 1900 - is best remembered as a tale about longing for home, about making do on one's own resources. In its light-hearted and fabulous way, Oz - like Wonderland - is a showplace of strangeness and oddity. (Indeed, the word odds comes close to sounding like Oz). But Oz - in this instance like Wonderland and Middle-earth both - is the product of a singular keen imagination churning away at a specific moment of a nation's cultural history. While Oz was being invented and charted by Baum at the turn of the twentieth century, the American experiment in democracy was coming to resemble, in ways both bad and good, a great and powerful empire.

The original depiction of Oz has always had something of a paste-board artificiality to it: both intentionally and, perhaps, unthinkingly, too. The story has real heart (that is why it has lasted) while playing with the notion of fake hearts, false courage, shoddy thinking. And the famous Wizard of Oz, a good-hearted humbug, presides over all: feckless, opportunistic, and skilled at flimflammery. (His sort is sadly not as far removed from our experience as we might like.) In Baum's novel, and also in the musical, *WICKED*, the brilliance and allure of the Emerald City is assured, since visitors and citizens alike don green-tinted glasses. Appearance and reality; glamour and grunge; seeming and being; patriot and traitor; propaganda and its

Protestors for the Women's Suffrage movement

nemesis, the wild scandal of truth. Wizardic leaders of any political stripe work most efficiently within the confines of binary systems, where subtler apprehensions and inconvenient distinctions are ruled out.

Much has been made about Baum's possible intention to comment on the turn-of-the-twentieth century discussion about currency standards. Baum had been a newspaper editor in the decade before he wrote his breakthrough novel. Did Baum invent the yellow brick road to endorse the gold standard as the suitable foundation for the nation's currency? Is the Tin Woodman intended to represent the automated worker: denatured, mechanized? Henry Ford's innovation, the factory assembly line, would after all become a reality in the next generation. I've always been inclined to suppose that if Baum was inspired by political cartoons to use silver, tin, straw and gold as motifs, he charmed the original significance out of them. Those symbols became themselves rich in their own invented meanings - arguably one of the themes of the novel, as it happens.

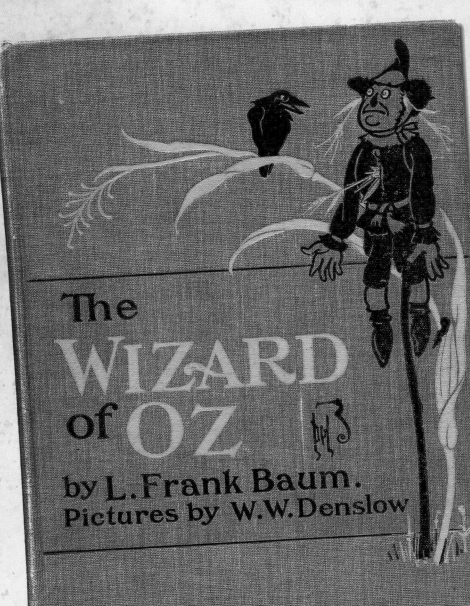

If Baum wasn't covertly supporting the populist campaign of William Jennings Bryant for the presidency in 1900 - and quite likely he was not - he does prove himself overtly political on another heated social issue of the day: the question of women's suffrage. His Oz is a matriarchy, with Witches good and bad ruling the country, and the encircled Wizard more or less imprisoned in his emerald tower. Dorothy arrives, we're told, and at quite a clip she does away with first one evil witch and then her wicked sister. Eventually - in later novels - the child Ozma, Pallas Athena by way of Shirley Temple, arises to govern wisely and well, if lacking much by way of a loyal opposition.

More seasoned fans of Oz aren't surprised to learn that Baum's mother-in-law, Matilda Gage, was a leading supporter of women's rights. Baum admired his mother-in-law, who was diligently at work on her magnum opus while living under Baum's roof. According to Baum's biographer, Katharine M. Rogers, Matilda Gage wrote in her 1893 publication, Woman, Church and State: A Historical Account of the Status of Woman through the Christian Ages with Reminiscences of the Matriarchate, "we have abundant proof that the so-called 'witch' was among the most profoundly scientific persons of the age."

New fans of Oz - even the ones who come to know the country through the musical play called WICKED or the novel that inspired it -aren't bedeviled by the notion that the Wicked Witch of the West is a powerhouse of a student, a political agitator against social oppression and misinformation, and a belter to boot.

(continued)

The story of *WICKED* relies on some of the same conventions explored by Baum's novel and made even more famous by the 1939 MGM film, *The Wizard of Oz*. WICKED spends no time on the question of currency. Nor does it seek to replace, reinterpret, or parody the bank of iconic images that Baum generated and that, in their new setting, dazzle even brighter. *WICKED* revisits the notions of social obligation and personal courage for a new and somewhat flummoxed generation, at a time when trust in government leadership is questioned more often than not.

Martin Green, professor of English who worked most of his life at Tufts University outside of Boston, often cited Robinson Crusoe as an eminent "foundation myth" of the character of both American and English societies. With innate dignity the isolate, thrown on his own resources, struggles to survive in a world that, while devoid of overt supernatural assistance, is not lacking in challenges and opportunities. The Wizard of Oz, a less significant work, nonetheless appears to serve a similar function in the American psyche. Crusoe came to be regarded as suitable for young readers; The Wizard of Oz was written expressly for them. If we take our myths early, like childhood innoculations, they may have a lifelong impact.

Dorothy, like Crusoe, is washed ashore on foreign soil. By dint of pluck and luck alike, and buoyed up by a natural inclination toward open-mindedness and good-heartedness, both castaways survive their ordeals. Perhaps they even thrive. Certainly they are altered forever for having met a challenge they never sought. They return to their points of departure - the grey plains of Kansas, the teaming London a decade after Pepys described it in his diary - changed for good. Did anyone believe their wild tales? If even they themselves wondered, 'Could all this have really happened to me?' they could not have been much diminished to learn that the answer was no. "The consolation of the imaginary is not imaginary consolation." Which is why we make such journeys in the first place.

--*Gregory Maguire*

Established as an Italian Restaurant since 1892

A traditional family run Italian Restaurant has become a favourite haunt for locals and visitors. Excellent value with friendly and efficient service.

316a Vauxhall Bridge Road London SW1V 1AA ★ For reservations call: 020 7834 5270

Opening Hours:
Monday - Saturday
12noon - 3.00pm & 5.00pm - 11.15pm
Closed Sundays and Bank Holidays
www.ilpostovictoria.co.uk

Kerry Ellis

Ristorante L'Arco

79 Buckingham Palace Road, London SW1W 0QJ T:020 7834 11 51

L'Arco Italian Restaurant is a Wicked pre & post-show dining experience!

Receive a warm welcome at our family-run restaurant, and enjoy delicious Italian specialities in a cosy atmosphere. Only a few minutes' walk from the Apollo Theatre, L'Arco is open later than any other restaurant in the area, making it the perfect place to continue your evening's events.

Lunch: 12.00pm – 3.00pm
Dinner: 5.30pm – 11.30pm
www.larco.co.uk

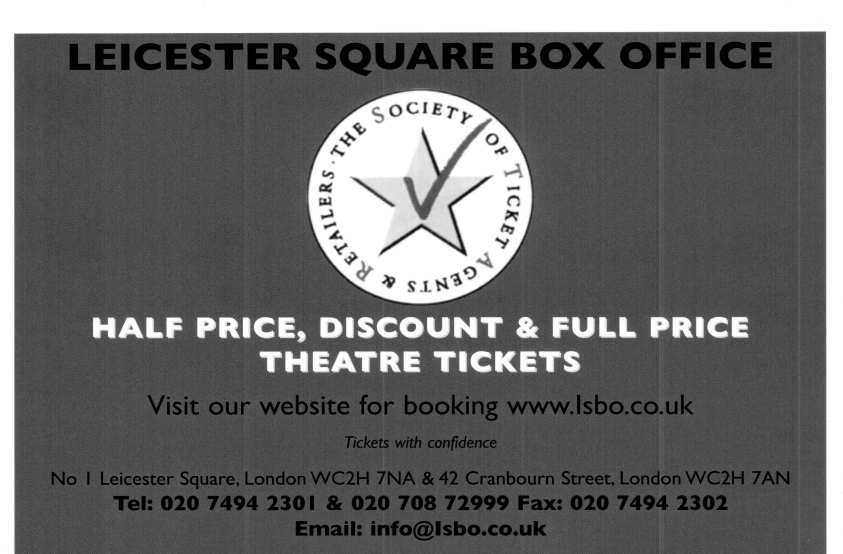

LEICESTER SQUARE BOX OFFICE

HALF PRICE, DISCOUNT & FULL PRICE THEATRE TICKETS

Visit our website for booking www.lsbo.co.uk

Tickets with confidence

No 1 Leicester Square, London WC2H 7NA & 42 Cranbourn Street, London WC2H 7AN
**Tel: 020 7494 2301 & 020 708 72999 Fax: 020 7494 2302
Email: info@lsbo.co.uk**

All offers subject to availability on the day

Dianne Pilkington

'THIS HEART-STOPPING SHOW IS A MUST-SEE'

MAIL ON SUNDAY

★★★★★

'PURE MAGIC'

SUNDAY EXPRESS

MUSIC BY
ELTON JOHN

BOOK & LYRICS BY
LEE HALL

DIRECTED BY
STEPHEN DALDRY

BILLY ELLIOT
THE MUSICAL

VICTORIA PALACE THEATRE · 0870 895 5577

www.billyelliotthemusical.com

CONTAINS SOME STRONG LANGUAGE

PRESENTED BY WORKING TITLE AND OLD VIC PRODUCTIONS IN ASSOCIATION WITH TIGER ASPECT. BASED ON THE UNIVERSAL PICTURES/STUDIO CANAL FILM © Billy London Ltd 2004

Oliver Tompsett

Creative Team

STEPHEN SCHWARTZ
Music/Lyrics

Stephen has contributed music and/or lyrics to *Godspell; Pippin; The Magic Show; The Baker's Wife; Working* (which he also adapted and directed); *Rags* and *Children of Eden*. For films, he collaborated with Alan Menken on the songs for Disney's *Enchanted*, as well as the animated features *Pocahontas* and *The Hunchback of Notre Dame*, and wrote songs for the DreamWorks animated feature *The Prince of Egypt*. He has released two CDs of new songs entitled *Reluctant Pilgrim* and *Uncharted Territory* available at www. stephenschwartz.com. Mr. Schwartz is also the artistic director of the ASCAP Musical Theatre Workshops and a member of the Dramatists Guild Council. Awards include three Academy Awards, four Grammy Awards, a star on the Hollywood Walk of Fame and a tiny handful of tennis trophies.

WINNIE HOLZMAN
Book

Winnie received a Tony nomination and a Drama Desk Award for *WICKED*. For television: created *My So-Called Life* (Emmy nomination). Also wrote for *thirtysomething* (WGA Award nomination) and executive produced (again with Marshall Herskovitz and Edward Zwick) *Once and Again* starring Sela Ward. For theatre: *Birds of Paradise* (with composer David Evans). For features: *'Til There Was You*. Ms. Holzman can be seen in *Jerry Maguire* (if you look really close). She lives in Los Angeles with her husband, actor Paul Dooley. She is a graduate of Princeton University and the New York University Musical Theatre Programme.

JOE MANTELLO
Director

Joe's directing credits include *November; The Receptionist; The Ritz; Blackbird; Three Days of Rain; The Odd Couple; Glengarry Glen Ross; Assassins* (Tony Award); *Take Me Out* (Tony Award) in London and New York; *Frankie and Johnny in the Clair de Lune; A Man of No Importance; Design for Living;* Terrence McNally and Jake Heggie's *Dead Man Walking* for the San Francisco Opera; *The Vagina Monologues; bash* (also at the Almeida Theatre in London); *Another American: Asking and Telling; Love! Valour! Compassion!; Proposals; The Mineola Twins; Corpus Christi; Mizlansky/Zilinsky or Schmucks; Blue Window; God's Heart; The Santaland Diaries; Lillian; Snakebit; Three Hotels; Imagining Brad* and *Fat Men in Skirts.* Mr. Mantello also directed the film *Love! Valour! Compassion!*. As an actor he appeared in *Angels in America* (Tony nomination) and *The Baltimore Waltz.* Mr. Mantello is a recipient of the Outer Critics Circle, Drama Desk, Lucille Lortel, Helen Hayes, Clarence Derwent, Obie and Joe A. Callaway awards. He is a member of Naked Angels and an associate artist at the Roundabout.

WAYNE CILENTO
Musical Staging

Broadway: *Sweet Charity* (Tony nomination); *Aida; The Who's Tommy* (Tony, Drama Desk, Astaire awards); *How to Succeed…* (Tony nomination); *Dream: The Johnny Mercer Musical* (Director and Choreographer; Tony nomination, Best Choreography); *Jerry's Girls; Baby* (Tony nomination). West End: *The Who's Tommy* (Olivier Award nomination). Other credits: Off-Broadway's *A Hot Minute* and *Angry Housewives;* the national tour of *Spirit;…Forum* at La Jolla (San Diego Drama Critics and Drama-Logue awards). Credits as a performer include *A Chorus Line* (Mike, original cast); *The Act; Seesaw; Perfectly Frank; Irene; Big Deal; Rachel Lily Rosenbloom* and Bob Fosse's *Dancin'* (Tony nomination). Mr. Cilento has done musical staging for Liza Minnelli, Barry Manilow, Chita Rivera, Billy Joel, Donna Summer and Pete Townshend.

EUGENE LEE
Scenic Designer

Eugene Lee holds BFA degrees from the Art Institute of Chicago and Carnegie Mellon University, an MFA from Yale School of Drama, and three honorary doctorates. He has been the production designer at NBC's *Saturday Night Live* since 1974. Film work includes Coppola's *Hammet;* Huston's *Mr. North;* and Malle's *Vanya on 42nd Street.* He has received the Tony Award, American Theatre Wing's Design Award, Outer Critics' Circle Award, Drama Desk Award, Lucille Lortel Award, Elliot Norton Award for Sustained Achievement, and Pell Award. He was recently inducted into the Theater Hall Fame in New York. In 2007, he received the Theatregoers' Choice Award for *WICKED* here in London. Other recent work in London includes *Drunk Enough to Say I Love You* at the Royal Court. He is a visiting professor at Brown University, and lives with his wife Brooke in Providence, where they raised their two sons.

SUSAN HILFERTY
Costume Designer

Susan has designed over 300 productions for theatres across America and internationally. London: sets and costumes for Athol Fugard's *My Children! My Africa!; A Place with the Pigs* (National Theatre); *Valley Song* at the Royal Court; *Playland* (Donmar Warehouse); *Sorrows and Rejoicings* (Tricycle) and costumes for August Wilson's *Jitney* (National Theatre). Directorial collaborators include Robert Falls, Richard Nelson, the late Garland Wright, Mark Lamos, Frank Galati, Des McAnuff, Marion McClinton, Laurie Anderson, Tony Kushner, Garry Hynes, and David Jones. Recent work: *Spring Awakening* (Tony nomination); *Lestat* (Tony nomination); *Assassins; Into the Woods* (Hewes Award, Tony and Drama Desk nominations); *Manon* (L.A. Opera, Berlin Staatsoper). Trained at Yale, she designs for opera, film, TV and dance, and chairs the Department of Design for Stage and Film at NYU Tisch. Her many awards include 2004 Tony, Drama Desk and Outer Critics Circle awards and an Olivier nomination for *WICKED.*

KENNETH POSNER
Lighting Designer

West End: *Hairspray; WICKED* (Olivier nominations) and *Sideman.* On Broadway over 30 plays and musicals including: *Coast of Utopia - Shipwreck* (Tony, Drama Desk and Outer Critics Circle Award); *Hairspray; Dirty Rotten Scoundrels; The Adventures of Tom Sawyer* (Tony nominations); *The Homecoming; Legally Blonde; The Odd Couple; Glengarry Glen Ross; Little Women; The Frogs; Imaginary Friends; Swing!; Charlie Brown; The Goat; Uncle Vanya; The Lion in Winter; Little Me; A View from the Bridge; The Last Night of Ballyhoo; The Little Foxes;* and *The Rose Tattoo.* Opera credits include designs for the New York City Opera and the Chicago Symphony Orchestra. Recipient of the OBIE for sustained excellence in lighting design. He resides in Verona, New Jersey with his wife Michelle and their three children.

TONY MEOLÁ
Sound Designer

Broadway credits include *The Ritz; Laugh Whore; Man of La Mancha; Sweet Smell of Success; Copenhagen; Kiss Me, Kate; Footloose; The Lion King* (Drama Desk Award); *The Sound of Music; Juan Darien; A Christmas Carol* (Madison Square Garden); *Steel Pier; A Funny Thing Happened on the Way to the Forum; The King and I; Moon Over Buffalo; Smokey Joe's Cafe; Guys and Dolls; Five Guys Named Moe; She Loves Me; The Red Shoes;* and *Anything Goes.* London includes *Kiss Me, Kate; The Lion King; Smokey Joe's Cafe;* and *Anything Goes.* National and international include *The Lion King; Les Misérables; Mozart; Der Gloeckner von Notre Dame.* Off-Broadway includes *Here Lies Jenny* and *The Normal Heart.* Tony is a graduate of Ithaca College's Department of Theatre Arts.

ELAINE J. McCARTHY
Projection Designer

Broadway: *Thurgood*; *Spamalot*; *Good Vibrations*; *After the Fall*; *Assassins*; *Man of La Mancha*; *Into the Woods*; *Judgment at Nuremberg*; *The Green Bird*. Off-Broadway: *Frequency Hopping* (set and projection); *Distracted* (set and projection); *Embedded*; *The Stendhal Syndrome*; *Suitcase*; *The Thing About Men*; *Speaking in Tongues*. Opera: *Dead Man Walking* (NYC Opera); *Mazeppa* and *War and Peace* (Kirov and Metropolitan Opera); Tan Dun's *The Gate*; Peter Sellar's *The Peony Pavilion*. Awards: 2003 Eddy Award.

TOM WATSON
Hair and Wig Designer

Tom Watson is head of the wig department at the Metropolitan Opera. He has designed wigs for more than 30 Broadway productions. Current and recent Broadway designs include *A Man for All Seasons*; *Sunday in the Park with George*; *South Pacific*; *Cyrano de Bergerac* and *A Tale of Two Cities*.

PIPPA AILION
Casting Director

Pippa has cast over 90 productions for West End, UK, US and globally. Seasons at Chichester, Crucible Theatre Sheffield & West Yorkshire Playhouse. She was Resident Associate Director and cast three seasons of 15 European Classics for Jonathan Miller at The Old Vic between 1987-1991. Current / recent West End: *Been So Long* (Young Vic); *Chess in Concert*; *Marguerite*; *The Drowsy Chaperone*; *Porgy & Bess*; WICKED; *Blue Man Group*; *Billy Elliot*; *We Will Rock You*; *The Lion King*. Future West End: *Legally Blonde*. Current Europe: *We Will Rock You*; *The Legend of The Lion King*; *Blue Man Group*. West End / London credits include: *I Love You Because*; *The Night of 1000 Voices*; *Generations*; *The Enchanted Pig*; *Six Dance Lessons in Six Weeks*; *Acorn Antiques* (& UK tour); *The Postman Always Rings Twice* (& WYPH); *Simply Heavenly*; *Follow My Leader*; *Slamdunk*; *Five Guys Named Moe*; *Tonight's the Night* (& UK tour); *Disney's Beauty and the Beast* (& tour); *Rent*; *Japes*; *Wit*; *The Magistrate*; *Hair*; *Into the Woods*. National Tours: *Riverdance*; *The Sunshine Boys*; *Jerry Springer The Opera*; *The Gingerbread Lady*.

STEPHEN OREMUS
Music Supervisor/Arrangements

Stephen is the Music Supervisor/Arranger of the original Broadway and subsequent worldwide productions of WICKED and *Avenue Q* (which he also orchestrated). For Broadway, he was also Music Supervisor, Vocal Arranger and Co-Orchestrator of All Shook Up and Vocal Arranger of *High Fidelity*. For off-Broadway, Stephen was Music Supervisor, Vocal Arranger and Orchestrator of *tick, tick... BOOM!* and Music Director of Andrew Lippa's *The Wild Party*. Other credits include Music Director of *Jerry Springer - The Opera* at Carnegie Hall; Music Director for Rufus Wainwright's re-creation of Judy Garland's famous 1961 concert at Carnegie Hall in New York City; the Hollywood Bowl in California; the Palladium in London and the Olympia in Paris; Music Director for the national tour of *Rent* and Music Supervisor and Vocal Arranger of *Signed, Sealed, Delivered - The Music of Stevie Wonder* starring Chaka Kahn in Las Vegas. Most recently, Stephen has been Music Supervisor and Arranger of the Los Angeles production of the Broadway-bound musical adaptation of *9 to 5*, which features an original score by Dolly Parton. He is a graduate of Berklee College of Music in Boston.

WILLIAM DAVID BROHN
Orchestrations

William received the 1998 Tony Award for Best Orchestrations for *Ragtime*. Other Broadway credits include *Curtains* (New York); *Mary Poppins* (London and New York); *Miss Saigon*; *The Secret Garden*; *Show Boat*; *Crazy for You*; *Carousel*; *Sweet Smell of Success*; *Oklahoma!*. In London: *Oliver!*; *The Witches of Eastwick*; *My Fair Lady* and *South Pacific*. He has provided arrangements for Marilyn Horne, James Galway, Placido Domingo and Joshua Bell's recent recording on Sony Classical of Bernstein's *West Side Story Suite* for Violin and Orchestra. William David Brohn is Orchestrator of *Oliver!* at the Theatre Royal Drury Lane.

JOEL FRAM
UK Music Supervisor

Joel has worked extensively in New York, conducting the Broadway productions of WICKED; *Sweet Smell of Success*; *The Music Man*; James Joyce's *The Dead*; *Jumpers* and *Cats*. U.S. national tours and regional credits include *Falsettos*; *Wonderful Town*; *My Fair Lady*; *A Little Night Music*; the American premiere of Alan Ayckbourn's *Dreams from a Summer House*; and the world premiere of two Andrew Lippa musicals: *The Little Princess* and *john & jen*. At New York's Symphony Space, he created the award-winning *New Voices* concert series and, for Stephen Sondheim's 75th birthday, co-produced and curated the 12-hour marathon *Wall to Wall Stephen Sondheim*. Mr. Fram has music directed two cast albums (*john & jen*; *A...My Name is Alice*), played with the New York Pops and the Boston Pops orchestras, restored several lost musicals for the acclaimed Encores! series, served on the musical theatre faculty of Yale, New York University, and the Danish Musical Academy, and is currently an Associate Music Supervisor for the Melbourne, Stuttgart and Tokyo productions of WICKED.

ALEX LACAMOIRE
Music Arrangements

Alex is the Music Director for *In The Heights*, which earned him a Drama Desk nomination for his orchestrations off-Broadway. In 2006 he music supervised and co-orchestrated *High Fidelity*, and for the year of 2005 he served as the Music Director of *Wicked* on Broadway. Other credits as Music Director, Arranger, Orchestrator and/or pianist: *Bat Boy: The Musical*; the 2001 Nat'l Tour of *Godspell*; Stephen Schwartz's *Captain Louie* and *Legally Blonde*.

JAMES LYNN ABBOTT
Dance Arrangements

Broadway: *Aida*; *Bombay Dreams*; *Rent*; *Footloose*; *Joseph and the Amazing Technicolor Dreamcoat*; *Cats*; *Sunset Boulevard* and *Miss Saigon*. National tours include *Starlight Express*; *Kiss of the Spider Woman*; *The Who's Tommy* and *Jesus Christ Superstar* among others. He has performed with Aretha Franklin, Dennis DeYoung of Styx, Shirley Bassey, Bob Hope and Vanessa Williams and with Elton John in "Greatest Hits Live" at Madison Square Garden. Clients include Dr Pepper, Frito Lay, American Airlines and General Electric.

LISA LEGUILLOU
US Associate Director

Lisa has also worked with Joe Mantello on *Frankie and Johnny in the Clair de Lune*; *Take Me Out* and *The Vagina Monologues*. She appeared in eight Broadway shows; on TV in *Sex and the City*; *NYPD Blue* and *NY Undercover*; and in the films *Changing Lanes*; *Center Stage*; *Everyone Says I Love You* and HBO's *Angels in America*.

MARK MYARS
Associate Choreographer

Mark is the Assistant Choreographer of WICKED's US National Tour, Chicago, Los Angeles, Japan, Germany and 2008's Australia productions. Broadway: Original Dance Captain of WICKED and *Footloose*. National: *Copacabana* ('Bolero Specialty'). Other: 'Carnival Boy' in Papermill's *Carousel*; 'Snowboy' in La Scala Opera's *West Side Story*; *Urban Cowboy* (workshop). Film: *Centerstage*; *The Producers*; *Across the Universe*. *West Side Story*-themed GAP ads. Many industrials as performer and choreographer.

EDWARD PIERCE
Associate Scenic Designer

Mr. Pierce operates a NYC-based design studio specializing in the production design of Broadway, touring, and international stage productions. With his team of artists, Edward provides first-class development and management of designs. Notable collaborations include the Tony Award-winning musical WICKED with Eugene Lee; *The Pirate Queen*; Elton John's *Aida*; *Ragtime*; *Cabaret*; *Noise/Funk* and *The Tempest*. www.edwardpierce.com

PETRA SINIAWSKI
UK Associate Director

West End credits have included leading roles in *Annie*; *On Your Toes*; *West Side Story* and *A Chorus Line*. She has appeared in television and films such as *The Music Lovers*; *The Boyfriend*; *Fiddler on the Roof*; *The Slipper and the Rose*; Frank Zappa's *200 Motels* and *Billy Elliot*. Petra has worked extensively both as a performer and choreographer in the repertory theatre, playing leads in *Chicago*; *Lulu*; *Bells Are Ringing*; *Stepping Out*; and *Blithe Spirit*. She has choreographed productions of *Jesus Christ Superstar*; *Hair*; *Poppy*; *Annie*; *King and I* and *Guys and Dolls* as well as directing *The Sound of Music*; *Sweet Charity*; and *West Side Story*. Petra has been Assistant and Resident Director on the West End musicals *Always*; *Annie*; *Kiss Me Kate*; *Ragtime* and *The Producers* and she directed the national tours of *Annie*; *Kiss Me Kate* and *The Producers* following their West End productions. She has assisted Susan Stroman, Michael Blakemore, Martin Charnin, Kathleen Marshall, Tommy Tune, Larry Fuller, Gillian Gregory, John Doyle, Frank Hauser and Thommie Walsh.

JAMES DRAISEY
Musical Director

James has worked extensively in theatre, as Musical Director, Musical Arranger and performer in both the West End and ontour. His recent credits include: *Fame*; *Saturday Night Fever*; *The Rat Pack*; *Annie Get your Gun* and the UK premieres of *Footloose* and *A Swell Party*. James has appeared on various TV and radio shows and alongside artists as diverse as Kathryn Jenkins, The Drifters and David Essex. He's also a keen helicopter pilot - keep a watch out on a rooftop near you!

JOE DULUDE II
Makeup Designer

Inspired by monster makeup as a kid, Joe is the designer for all WICKED productions. Broadway: *Grease!* revival; *The Wedding Singer*; *Assassins*; *Into the Woods* (key makeup Vanessa Williams). Off-Broadway: *Birdie*; *Broadway Bares* (design and body-painting). Film and Television: *E!*; *Style*; *Lifetime*; PBS; *Access Hollywood*; MTV. Print and Runway: *Vanity Fair*, *Marie Claire*, *Vibe*, *Rolling Stone*, Diesel, Enyce, and more. Other: Artist Relations and Consultant for MAC Cosmetics.

GREGORY MAGUIRE
Author of Original Novel

Gregory had written a dozen novels for children before launching his first adult novel, *Wicked*. A devotee of children's fantasy, Maguire's subsequent novels for adults are variations-on-a-theme: *Confessions of an Ugly Stepsister* considers Cinderella as a seventeenth-century maid from Haarlem; *Lost* evokes the ghost of Charles Dickens' Scrooge; and *Mirror Mirror* concerns a High Renaissance Snow White trapped in a household governed by the scheming Borgias. Gregory Maguire's novel *Wicked* is now followed by two subsequent volumes in The Wicked Years sequence: *Son of a Witch* and *A Lion Among Men*.

RICHARD BULLIMORE
Production Manager

Richard trained at LAMDA. His career in theatre started with Stage Sixty at Theatre Royal, Stratford East, followed by a period touring with a wide variety of shows. He was asked to join the production department of the National Theatre Company at the Old Vic, under the Artistic Directorship of Laurence Olivier, and during his seven year tenure worked on upwards of 50 productions. Following the move into the new building on the South Bank, Richard worked as Production Manager for the Olivier Theatre. He left the National to set up The Production Office, offering production management and technical services to commercial producers. During this time, he worked on some of London's leading musicals: *Cats; Starlight Express; They're Playing Our Song; Mutiny* and many others. He then returned to the National as Technical Director under the Artistic Directorship of Richard Eyre. Subsequently, he has returned to the West End working on shows such as *Crazy for You; Jesus Christ Superstar; Whistle Down the Wind; Saturday Night Fever; The King & I; Fosse; Chitty Chitty Bang Bang; Bombay Dreams; Matthew Bourne's Nutcracker; Absolutely! {perhaps}; The Producers; Sinatra at the London Palladium;* the recent revival of *Evita* and now *WICKED*.

ACT PRODUCTIONS
NICK SALMON & NIA JANIS
General Management

Act is a leading West End Producer and General Manager. Current and recent productions include: *Marguerite* directed by Jonathan Kent (Theatre Royal Haymarket); *Crown Matrimonial* directed by David Grindley (Yvonne Arnaud Theatre, Guildford and UK tour); *WICKED* (Apollo Victoria); *Boeing-Boeing* directed by Matthew Warchus (Comedy, Broadway and UK tour); Tim Supple's *A Midsummer Night's Dream* (Roundhouse, UK, Australian and US tours); *Happy Days* directed by Deborah Warner (Brooklyn Academy of Music); *Ring Round the Moon* directed by Sean Mathias (Playhouse); the award-winning *Frost/Nixon* starring Frank Langella and Michael Sheen (Gielgud and Broadway); *Whipping It Up* starring Richard Wilson and Robert Bathurst (New Ambassadors); *A Voyage Round My Father* by John Mortimer starring Derek Jacobi (Wyndham's); *Sinatra at the London Palladium* directed by David Leveaux; *Edward Scissorhands* directed and choreographed by Matthew Bourne (Sadler's Wells, UK and Far East tour); *Epitaph for George Dillon* starring Joseph Fiennes and Francesca Annis directed by Peter Gill (Comedy); the Donmar Warehouse production of *Mary Stuart* directed by Phyllida Lloyd (Apollo); *Don Carlos* starring Derek Jacobi directed by Michael Grandage (Gielgud) and the Olivier Award-winning National Theatre's production of *Anything Goes* (Theatre Royal Drury Lane). www.actproductions.co.uk

321 THEATRICAL MANAGEMENT
US Management

Nina Essman, Nancy Nagel Gibbs and Marcia Goldberg's Broadway and off-Broadway management credits include: *WICKED* (Broadway, Chicago, Los Angeles, and national tour); *The 25th Annual Putnam County Spelling Bee* (Broadway, Chicago, and national tour); *STRIKING 12; Man of La Mancha; The Good Body* (national tour); *The Graduate* (Broadway and national tour); *The Vagina Monologues; Bat Boy; Fully Committed; The Search for Signs of Intelligent Life in the Universe; Lifegame; The Lion King; De La Guarda; Hank Williams: Lost Highway; Rent; Guys and Dolls; How to Succeed…; 42nd Street; I Love You, You're Perfect…; Visiting Mr. Green; Full Gallop; Smoke on the Mountain; The Santaland Diaries; Smokey Joe's Café* and *Family Secrets*.

2008/09 London Company

THE CAST

(in order of appearance)

Glinda	DIANNE PILKINGTON
Witch's Father	ANDY MACE
Witch's Mother	RACHEL MULDOON
Midwife	AILEEN DONOHOE
Elphaba	KERRY ELLIS
Nessarose	CAROLINE KEIFF
Boq	JEREMY LEGAT
Madame Morrible	HARRIET THORPE
Doctor Dillamond	ANDY MACE
Fiyero	OLIVER TOMPSETT
The Wonderful Wizard of Oz	DESMOND BARRIT
Chistery	MATTHEW BOULTON

Monkeys, Students, Palace Guards, Denizens of the Emerald City and Other Citizens of Oz:
CINDY BELLIOT, MATTHEW BOULTON, SABRINA CARTER, NADINE COX, MATTHEW CROKE, AILEEN DONOHOE,
SARAH EARNSHAW, A.C. GARCIA, ASHLEIGH GRAY, ALEX JESSOP, PIPPA LLOYD, RACHEL MULDOON, SEAN PARKINS,
JAKE SAMUELS, DAVID STOLLER, LIAM TAMNE, LINDSAY TAYLOR, EMILY TIERNEY, HANNAH TOY, GEORGE URE

Standby for Elphaba: ASHLEIGH GRAY; Standby for Glinda: SARAH EARNSHAW

Understudy for Elphaba: SABRINA CARTER; for Glinda: PIPPA LLOYD;
for Fiyero: LIAM TAMNE, JAKE SAMUELS; for the Wonderful Wizard of Oz: ANDY MACE, DAVID STOLLER;
for Madame Morrible: NADINE COX, AILEEN DONOHOE; for Dr. Dillamond: DAVID STOLLER, TIM WALTON;
for Nessarose: KADY-JO JACKSON, EMILY TIERNEY; for Boq: ALEX JESSOP, GEORGE URE

Swings: KADY-JO JACKSON, KEELEY JANE JACKSON, AIMEE LEWIS, MITCHELL MAHONY, ADAM MURRAY, CHLOE TAYLOR, TIM WALTON, GARY WOOD

Resident Dance Supervisor: ADAM MURRAY
Assistant Dance Captains: KADY-JO JACKSON, HANNAH TOY

Company Manager	Sophie Gabszewicz
Stage Manager	Anthony Field
Deputy Stage Manager	Becky Timbrell
Assistant Stage Manager	Zoe Attridge
Assistant Stage Manager	Luciano Macis
Assistant Stage Manager	Rachel Tiley

Opening Night 27th September 2006   The show runs for 2 HOURS 50 MINUTES with one 20 minute interval.

MUSICAL NUMBERS

ACT I

"No One Mourns the Wicked"	Glinda and Citizens of Oz
"Dear Old Shiz"	Students
"The Wizard and I"	Morrible, Elphaba
"What is this Feeling?"	Galinda, Elphaba, and Students
"Something Bad"	Dr. Dillamond and Elphaba
"Dancing through Life"	Fiyero, Galinda, Boq, Nessarose, Elphaba and Students
"Popular"	Galinda
"I'm Not That Girl"	Elphaba
"One Short Day"	Elphaba, Glinda and Denizens of the Emerald City
"A Sentimental Man"	The Wizard
"Defying Gravity"	Elphaba, Glinda, Guards and Citizens of Oz

ACT II

"No One Mourns the Wicked" (Reprise)	Citizens of Oz
"Thank Goodness"	Glinda, Morrible and Citizens of Oz
"The Wicked Witch of the East"	Elphaba, Nessarose and Boq
"Wonderful"	The Wizard and Elphaba
"I'm Not That Girl" (Reprise)	Glinda
"As Long as You're Mine"	Elphaba and Fiyero
"No Good Deed"	Elphaba
"March of the Witch Hunters"	Boq and Citizens of Oz
"For Good"	Glinda and Elphaba
"Finale"	All

THE ORCHESTRA

Musical Director / Conductor: James Draisey
Assistant Musical Director: Mark Etherington

Violin / Mandolin: Julian Leaper; Cello: Bozidar Vukotic; Piccolo / Flute / Alto Flute / Soprano Recorder in C: Rebecca Larsen; Oboe / English Horn / Penny Whistle: Nicky Holland; Soprano Sax / Eb Clarinet / Bb Clarinet / Bass Clarinet: Paul Saunders; Trumpet / Flugel Horn: Andy Greenwood; Trumpet / Flugel Horn: Danny Marsden; Tenor Trombone / Bass Trombone: Ed Tarrant; French Horn: Marcus Bates; Electric Guitar / Nylon Acoustic / Banjo / 12 string: Andy Phillip; Double Bass / 5 String Electric / Fretless Electric: Don Richardson; Drums: Guy Richman; Percussion: Daniel Ellis; Keyboard 1: Peter Whinnett; Keyboard 2: Mark Etherington; Keyboard 3: Gareth Ellis; Keyboard 4: Paul Frankish

Orchestral Management: Maurice Cambridge for Accord Music Productions Ltd.

Kerry Ellis

Dianne Pilkington

Dianne Pilkington and Kerry Ellis

Cast

KERRY ELLIS
Elphaba

Kerry trained at Laine Theatre Arts. Theatre includes: 'Svetlana' in *Chess In Concert* at the Royal Albert Hall; 'Fantine' in *Les Misérables* at the Queen's Theatre and 'Ellen' in the national tour of *Miss Saigon*. She created the role of 'Meat' in the Queen/Ben Elton musical *We Will Rock You* at the Dominion Theatre and took part in the Queen's Golden Jubilee Concert at Buckingham Palace. Kerry understudied the role of 'Eliza Dolittle' in Trevor Nunn's production of *My Fair Lady* at the National Theatre and Drury Lane, playing the role opposite Jonathan Pryce on many occasions. Workshops include *Way Beyond Blue*, written by Imogen Stubbs and directed by Trevor Nunn, and the title role in *Helen of Troy*, directed by Gary Griffin. More recently, Kerry released her debut CD recording *Wicked In Rock*, produced by Brian May, which is available at this theatre and on iTunes. Kerry was honoured to be invited to perform 'Defying Gravity' with Brian May at the 2008 *Royal Variety Performance*. Kerry returns to the role of 'Elphaba' in the London production of *WICKED*, having played the role for the past six months at the Gershwin Theatre on Broadway. www.kerryellis.co.uk

OLIVER TOMPSETT
Fiyero

Oliver made his professional and West End debut in October 2002 in the Madness/Tim Firth musical *Our House*, directed by Matthew Warchus, at London's Cambridge Theatre. His subsequent London stage appearances include: Benny Andersson and Björn Ulvaeus' *Mamma Mia!*, directed by Phyllida Lloyd, at the Prince of Wales Theatre; *Notes From New York* at the Trafalgar Studios and *Christmas In New York* at the Apollo Theatre, both directed by David Randall; 'Caliph' in *Kismet*, directed by Tiffany Watt-Smith, at the Arcola Theatre and 'Harry Lytton' in Richard Stirling's *Over My Shoulder: The Story of Jessie Matthews*, directed by Stewart Nicholls, at Wyndham's Theatre. Immediately prior to joining the original cast of *WICKED*, in September 2006, Oliver appeared in Trevor Nunn's production of Peter Shaffer's *The Royal Hunt of the Sun* at the National Theatre. He has twice appeared on *The Royal Variety Performance*, in 2002 and 2006. He trained at the Arts Educational School. Alongside Oliver's acting career he is also an accomplished Singer/Songwriter, and his debut album, *Sentimental Heart*, is a mix of Soul, Pop and Rock that demonstrates his versatility as a vocalist. Copies of the CD are available from the merchandise kiosks in the theatre.

www.myspace.com/olivertompsett or www.OliverTompsett.com.

HARRIET THORPE
Madame Morrible

Harriet is best known for her roles as 'Carole' in the BBC's popular *Brittas Empire*, and as 'Fleur' in *Absolutely Fabulous*. More recently she played opposite Jason Donovan as 'Mrs Lovett' in John Doyle's *Sweeney Todd* and as 'Fraulein Kost' in Rufus Norris' West End production of *Cabaret*. Work with Dawn French and Jennifer Saunders includes: *Girls on Top; French & Saunders* series and most recently *Vivienne Vyle*. Other TV includes: *Midsomer Murders; Casualty; Doctors* and *The Bill*. Theatre includes: several seasons at the National Theatre, in the Richard Eyre and David Hare company in *Pravda* and *The Government Inspector*, Howard Davies' production of *All My Sons* and *A Prayer For Owen Meany*. Her West End credits include: 'Madame Thenardier' in *Les Misérables; The Vagina Monologues* and *Jackie O*. At Regent's Park parts include: 'Titania' in *A Midsummer Night's Dream;* 'Maria' in *Twelfth Night;* the 'Queen' in *Cymbeline;* and at the Young Vic, Timothy Sheader's *Street Car to Tennessee*. At the Almeida she played 'Ida Arnold' in Michael Attenborough's *Brighton Rock*. Films include: Merchant Ivory's *Maurice; Greystroke;* Mike Leigh's *Life is Sweet;* Zefferelli's *Toscanini; Suzie Gold* and the Head of the W.I. in *Calendar Girls*. She has recently completed filming *The Calling* and a new horror film, *S.N.U.B.*

DESMOND BARRIT
The Wonderful Wizard of Oz

Theatre includes *The History Boys; Stuff Happens; A Funny Thing Happened On The Way To The Forum; Mountain Giants; The Recruiting Officer; The Wind in the Willows; Three Men on a Horse; Jacobowsky and the Colonel; The Magistrate* (National Theatre); 'Falstaff' in *Henry IV Parts 1 & 2* (Olivier nomination); *A Midsummer Night's Dream* (Helen Hayes Award); *The Comedy of Errors* (Olivier Award); *King Lear; The Man Who Came to Dinner; The Tempest* (Clarence Derwent Award); *Twelfth Night; Macbeth; The Constant Couple* (RSC); *The History Boys; Accidental Death of an Anarchist; Real Inspector Hound/Black Comedy; Dubarry; The Scarlett Pimpernel; Eurydice; Three Men on a Horse; The Lair; A View from the Bridge; This is a Chair; Then Again; The Chinese Wolf; The Three Musketeers; HMS Pinafore;* and *Twelfth Night* (London); *The Merchant of Venice; On the Razzle; Fortune's Fool* (Chichester); *My Fair Lady* (Hollywood Bowl). TV includes *Northangar Abbey; Young King Arthur; Midsomer Murders; The Bill; Follow the Star; Madame Bovary; Maxwell's House; The Old Devils; Homer and His Pigeons; Boon; Pirates II; Dalziel and Pascoe; Miracles Extra; True Tilda; Poirot*. Films include *Oliver Twist; A Christmas Carol; Alice Through the Looking Glass; Rebecca's Daughters; A Midsummer Night's Dream; All for Love; Daylight Robbery.*

DIANNE PILKINGTON
Glinda

Dianne trained at Guildford School of Acting. Theatre credits: 'Grizabella' in *Cats* (national tour); 'Belinda' in *The Far Pavilions* (Shaftesbury Theatre); 'Mary' in *Tonight's the Night* (Victoria Palace); 'Belle' in Disney's *Beauty and the Beast* (national tour); 'Kim' in the original cast of Boy George's new musical *Taboo;* the title role in *Snow White and the Seven Dwarves* at the Victoria Palace Theatre, opposite Lily Savage; 'Protestant Girl' in *The Beautiful Game* (Cambridge Theatre); 'The Beggar Woman' in *Sweeney Todd* (Bridewell Theatre); 'Marion' in *Tess* (Savoy Theatre) and understudied and played 'Fantine' and 'Cosette' in *Les Misérables* (Palace Theatre). Original Cast Recordings: *Taboo, The Beautiful Game, Tonight's The Night.* Other credits include 'Hope' in the London workshop production of *Urinetown,* directed by John Rando; 'Tonya' in the workshop of *Dr Zhivago* directed by Des McAnuff; the title role in *Helen of Troy* - a new musical, directed by Gary Griffin; 'Charlotte' in *Charlotte - Life or Theatre?* and appearing with *Boy George in Concert* at the Albert Hall. Dianne has recently finished filming *The Wolf Man* opposite Benecio Del Toro, for Universal Pictures due for release in 2009.

CAROLINE KEIFF
Nessarose

JEREMY LEGAT
Boq

ANDY MACE
Doctor Dillamond, Witch's Father

Caroline graduated with a First Class BA (Hons) from the Guildford School of Acting. Caroline was in the original London cast of *WICKED*, has understudied and performed the role of 'Glinda' and is now thrilled to be playing 'Nessarose'. Previous credits include 'Alice' in *The Far Pavilions* (Shaftesbury Theatre); 'Sarah Brown' in *Guys and Dolls* (Courtyard Theatre); 'Chiffon' in *The Little Shop of Horrors* (Jersey Opera House); 'Thea Elvsted' in Ibsen's *Hedda Gabler* (Norwich Playhouse); 'Sally Bowles' in *Cabaret* (Yvonne Arnaud Theatre); 'Anytime Annie' in *42nd Street* (Octagon Theatre, Yeovil); *Summer Holiday* (UK no. 1 tour) and 'Woman 1' in *Songs for a New World* (Guildford Playhouse). With *WICKED*, Caroline has appeared on *Blue Peter, Children In Need* and at the *Royal Variety Performance* (London Coliseum).

Jeremy trained at the Royal Academy of Dramatic Art. Most recently he reprised his Ian Charleson Award nominated performance as 'Cupid' in *Dido, Queen of Carthage* at Kensington Palace, a production originally performed at the Chapel of St. Barnabas, Soho. His other theatre credits include: 'John Darling' in the British theatrical premiere of Stiles and Drewe's musical adaptation of *Peter Pan* (Birmingham Rep); 'Jamie' in *Beautiful Thing* (Leicester Haymarket); 'Kay' in *The Snow Queen* (Brewhouse Theatre, Taunton); 'Herb' in *Who's Afraid of the Big Bad Book* (Soho Theatre); 'Moritz Steifel' in *Spring Awakening* (Young Vic/Jerwood Foundation); 'White Steve' in the British premiere of Adam Rapp's *Gompers* (Arcola Theatre); and 'Dipper' in *Oliver!* (London Palladium). Jeremy's film and television appearances include: *Hustle; The Sinking of Estonia; Hope and Glory* (BBC); 'Jason Bassett' in *Mike Bassett: Manager* (ITV); *Endgame* (Evolution Films) and most recently 'Christopher Whitehouse' in *Filth: The Mary Whitehouse Story.*

Andy made his West End debut in Boublil and Schönberg's *Martin Guerre,* directed by Declan Donellan at the Prince Edward Theatre in which he played both 'Father Dominic' and 'Guillaume' on many occasions. His other recent West End credits include: ensemble and 'Percival Glyde' in *The Woman In White;* 'Bishop of Digne', 'Lesgles' and 'Javert' in *Les Misérables;* 'Roger' and 'Mark' in *Rent* (2003); 'Teddy', 'Jerry' and 'Harold' in the Broadway musical version of *The Full Monty;* 'Radet' and 'Fouche' in *Napoleon,* directed by Francesca Zambello; 'Riff Raff' in Richard O'Brien's *The Rocky Horror Show;* 'Roger', 'Mark' and 'Steve' in *Rent* (1999); 'Aeneas' in *Troilus and Cressida;* 'Cobweb' in *A Midsummer Night's Dream* and 'Frank' and 'Coles' in *Gentlemen Prefer Blondes,* all at the Open Air Theatre, Regent's Park.

Ashleigh Gray

Sarah Earnshaw

Matthew Boulton

Cindy Belliot

Sabrina Carter

Nadine Cox

Matthew Croke

Aileen Donohoe

A.C. Garcia

Kady-Jo Jackson

Keeley Jane Jackson

Alex Jessop

Aimee Lewis

Pippa Lloyd

ASHLEIGH GRAY
(Standby for Elphaba)

Training: Guildford School of Acting. Graduating with the Principal's Award for Musical Theatre and the Margaret Veale Award for Singing. Theatre includes: 'Emily' in *Myths & Hymns* (European Premiere, Finborough Theatre); 'Miss Lynch', understudy 'Rizzo' & 'Jan' in *Grease* (UK Tour); 'The Administrator' in *NHS The Musical* (Theatre Royal, Plymouth); 'Kirsty' in *Only You Can Save Mankind* (Pleasance Theatre, Edinburgh) and 'Kim' in *Taboo* (UK Tour). Recordings include: *'Nicola'* in *In 2 Minds* (BBV Distribution) and a duet with Oliver Tompsett on *Sentimental Heart* (Avenue West Records). Other work includes: featured vocalist in several of the *Notes from New York* series (West End); *A Little House Music* (Arts Theatre); *West End and Hollywood Favourites* (Queens Theatre) and *The Magnificent Musicals with Ruthie Henshall* (UK Tour). www.ashleighgray.com

SARAH EARNSHAW
(Standby for Glinda)

Training: Mountview Academy Of Theatre Arts. Theatre includes: 'Mary O' Brien' in *A Girl Called Dusty* (Duchess Theatre, Workshop); understudy 'Alice/Queen Of Hearts' in *Alice in Wonderland* (West Yorkshire Playhouse); 'Carrie Pipperidge' in *Carousel* (Bridewell Theatre); *West End Stars in Concert* (Irish Tour); *Whistle Down The Wind* (Riverside Studios, NYMT) and *Annie* (George Square Theatre, Edinburgh, NYMT). Sarah was a member of the original West End cast of *WICKED*. Television includes: *The Royal Variety Performance* 2006; *Children In Need* and *Blue Peter* (All BBC). Recordings include: 'Tallula' in *Bugsy Malone* (BBC Radio 2).

CINDY BELLIOT
(Ensemble)

Training: Cindy Belliot completed her education at the Dance Academy Lucia Marthas in the Netherlands, where she received her Bachelor degree in Musical Theatre and her Bachelor degree in Teaching. Theatre includes: dance ensemble and understudy 'Nala' in Disney's musical *The Lion King* in The Netherlands in her third year at the Academy. In 2006 Cindy played 'Jemima' in *Cats* (Dutch tour), and 'Ella' in the English language musical *Bubbling Brown Sugar* (Dutch tour). Television includes: several Dutch television shows, including *Musicals in Ahoy, The Musical Awards* and many more. Film includes: 'Charley' in the Dutch movie *Feestje*. Cindy is very thankful for her first role in the West End in *WICKED*.

MATTHEW BOULTON
(Ensemble, Chistery)

Training: Northern Ballet School. Theatre includes: *Desperately Seeking Susan,* understudying 'Jay' and 'Alex' (Novello Theatre); *Footloose,* as alternate 'Ren McCormack' (UK Tour & Playhouse); *Mary Poppins* (Prince Edward); *Starlight Express,* playing 'Purse' and understudying 'Caboose' (original cast, UK Tour); *Tonight's The Night* understudying 'Bonehead' & 'Travolta' (original cast, Victoria Palace); *Fame* understudying 'Nick Piazza' and 'Goody' (Aldwych) and 'Magic Of The Musicals' (UK Tour). Recordings include: *Tonight's The Night* (original cast recording).

SABRINA CARTER
(Ensemble, Elphaba u/s)

Training: MA in Musical Theatre, Royal Scottish Academy of Music and Drama. Training credits include: 'Grace/Claudia' in *Elegies for Angels, Punks and Raging Queens;* 'Erica' in *Yeti – An Abominal Musical;* 'Kate Keller' in *All My Sons* and 'Joanne' in *Company.* Theatre includes: 'Clarinda' in *Clarinda - The Musical* (Netherbow Theatre, Edinburgh); 'Tigerlily' and 'Mrs Darling' in *Peter Pan* (Eden Court, Inverness); 'Charity' in *Guilt* (Upstairs at the Gatehouse, London); 'Princess So-Shy' in *Aladdin* (MacRobert) and 'Meg' in *Marrying Meg* (Highland Quest for a New Musical). Television includes: *Macmusical* for Endemol. Recordings include: *Clarinda OST.* Sabrina is delighted to be joining the cast of *WICKED.*

NADINE COX
(Ensemble, Madame Morrible u/s)

Training: Morgan Aslanoff School of Dance, Actors Centre, University College London, Sorbonne, Paris. Theatre includes: 'Mrs Bixby' in *Seven Brides For Seven Brothers* (UK Tour); understudy 'Georgie/Pam' in *The Full Monty* (original London cast); 'Judith' in *Elegies for Angels, Punks and Raging Queens* (Bridewell Theatre); 'Narrator' in *Joseph And His Amazing Technicolor Dreamcoat* (UK Tour); 'Mona Kent' in *Dames At Sea* (Prince Regent Theatre). Television: 'Mrs Capaldi' in *Rikki and Julie* (Romeo and Juliet Today, short film); *The Royal Variety Performance* 2006 and *Children In Need* for *WICKED* (BBC); Trudi and Lidl Supermarkets commercials. Recordings: *Elegies for Angels, Punks and Raging Queens* (London cast); backing/lead vocalist for JMusic. Other work: 'Mrs Anderson' in workshop of *Waiting for the Dawn* (Arts Theatre, West End). Radio: 'Delila/Mrs.T' in the *Dr. Who* audio, *The Ultimate Adventure.*

MATTHEW CROKE
(Ensemble)

Training: Maureen Law Theatre School/Sharon Berry School of Dance/Laine Theatre Arts. Theatre includes: *Peter Pan* (Grand Opera House, Belfast) understudying 'Hook'; *Cinderella* (New Wimbledon Theatre) understudying 'Prince Charming'; *Grease* (Piccadilly Theatre London) understudying 'Eugene'; *A Chorus Line* (Crucible Theatre, Sheffield) playing 'Roy' and understudying 'Larry'; *Lucky Stiff* playing the leading role of 'Harry Witherspoon' (LTA studios) and *An Evening with Val Doonican and Friends* performing as a featured artist (solo singer). Television includes: featured dancer in *A Royal Gala* as part of the opening of the Wales Millennium Centre (BBC); dancer in *The Royal Variety Performance* 2005 (Wales Millennium Centre, ITV/LWT) and a featured dancer in *Abbamania 2; Discomania 2* and *Elvismania* (Granada TV/ LWT). Matthew would like to thank his family and teachers for all their help and support.
www.kelly-management.com

AILEEN DONOHOE
(Ensemble, Madame Morrible u/s)

Training: Honours Degree in English Literature from Trinity College, Dublin and a Post-Graduate Diploma in Musical Theatre from The Royal Academy of Music. Theatre includes: *Mamma Mia!* (international tour); *The Phantom of the Opera* (Her Majesty's Theatre); *Beauty and the Beast* (UK No. 1 tour); *One Touch of Venus* (Linbury Studio, Royal Opera House); *The Count of Monte Cristo* (Player's Theatre); *Work* (Diorama Arts Centre, London); *Zip Goes A Million* (Theatre Museum, London); *Forgotten Broadway* (New York); *The Importance of Being Earnest* (Celtic Sounds, US Tour); *Amphibians* (Andrew's Lane Theatre, Dublin); *On Raftery's Hill* (Rosemary Branch Theatre). Television includes: Judy Garland in *Pick of the Fringe* (Channel 4); *Late Late Show* (RTE), *Good Morning TV* (TV3).

A.C. GARCIA
(Ensemble)

Training: A.C. trained at the Corraine Collins Dance Studio in Cheltenham before graduating from Laine Theatre Arts last year. Theatre includes: featured tap soloist in *Big Band Beat* (Tokyo Disney Resort); *The Name of the Game; Seeing Tomorrow; Believe in Yourself* (Epsom Playhouse); ensemble, understudied and played 'Dame Trot' in *Jack and the Beanstalk* (Richmond Theatre); ensemble and understudied 'Ugly Sisters' in *Cinderella* (Bexhill Pavilion) and was in a classical trio for the IDTA Annual Conference (Royal Lancaster Hotel). Television includes: dancer for *Abbamania 2* and *Madonnamania* (LWT) and a dancer and swing for *The Royal Variety Performance* 2004 and 2005. A.C would like to thank his mum, dad, wonderful family and friends, and Erin for all their love and continued support. He would like to dedicate his performance to his granddad.

KADY-JO JACKSON
(Swing, Nessarose u/s)

Training: Elizabeth Hill School of Dance & Drama and Laine Theatre Arts. Theatre includes: crossover swing, original London cast, *WICKED* (Apollo Victoria); ensemble in *Jack and the Beanstalk* (Birmingham Hippodrome); ensemble in *Oliver!* (Cameron Mackintosh Productions). Television includes: *The Royal Variety Performance* (Coliseum); *Children In Need* and *Blue Peter* (BBC). Kady-Jo is thrilled to be continuing her journey in Oz, and would like to thank her loving parents and partner Mike for everything.

KEELEY JANE JACKSON
(Swing)

Training: Elizabeth Hill School of Dance & Drama and Laine Theatre Arts. Theatre includes: understudy 'Rhoda' in Irving Berlin's Broadway Production *White Christmas* (Edinburgh Playhouse & Cardiff Millennium Centre); understudy 'Ice Queen', *Santa Claus The Musical* (Mayflower Southampton & Liverpool Empire); 'Connie Burelli'. *The Ratpack Live From Las Vegas* (original cast UK & European tour); lead vocalist with P&O'S Stadium Theatre Company 'MV Arcadia' (World Cruise); Standby 'Dorothy', *Wizard Of Oz* (St. Albans Arena & Richmond Theatre). Television includes: *Grease Is The Word; Knight's School* (ITV); *I'd Do Anything; Children In Need; Blue Peter* (BBC). Other work includes: 'Heather Langenkamp' for workshop production of *Bloodbath The Musical,* a new musical by Tony McHale. Keeley would like to thank her Mum, Dad, Kady-Jo & Craig for their constant love and support.

ALEX JESSOP
(Ensemble, Boq u/s)

Training: Laine Theatre Arts. Theatre includes: 'Eddie' and understudy 'Sky' in *Mamma Mia!* (international tour); 'Drill Sergeant/Sergeant O'Leary' in *Movin' Out* (Apollo Victoria Theatre); 'Bobby C' and alternate 'Tony Manero' in *Saturday Night Fever* (Apollo Victoria Theatre and UK Tour); ensemble and understudy 'Galileo' in *We Will Rock You* (Dominion Theatre) and swing and understudy 'Amos Heart' in *Chicago* (Adelphi Theatre). Television includes: *Dick Whittington* and *Aladdin,* featured dancer and Assistant Choreographer for LWT. Other work includes: *Christmas in New York* (Lyric Theatre), featured vocalist as part of the *Notes from New York* series.

AIMEE LEWIS
(Swing)

Training: Performers College, specialising in Dance Theatre. Theatre includes: *The Wizard of Oz* for Spillers Pantomimes (Woodville Halls Theatre, Gravesend) and *The Spirit of Christmas* (US Tour) with The Osmonds. Television includes: *Top of the Pops* for Sam and Mark and Peter Andre and *Doctor Who: Daleks in Manhattan.* Other work includes: numerous trade shows in and around London, including The Savoy, Grosvenor House and Dorchester hotels.

PIPPA LLOYD
(Ensemble, Glinda u/s)

Training: Royal Scottish Academy of Music & Drama. Theatre includes: *After Liverpool* (Kings Head Theatre); *Bash* (Barons Court Theatre); *Jenufa* (Arcola Theatre); *Subway* (Sheraton Hotel, Korea); *Achilles In Heels* (Landor Theatre); *Far From The Madding Crowd* (Cardiff Musical Theatre/Edinburgh Festival) and *The Art of the Fugue* (Bedlam Theatre). Television includes: promotional video for Gala Bingo. Other work includes: rehearsed reading for *Dawlish Road* (Soho Theatre).

Mitchell Mahony   Rachel Muldoon   Adam Murray   Sean Parkins   Jake Samuels   David Stoller   Liam Tamne

Chloe Taylor   Lindsay Taylor   Emily Tierney   Hannah Toy   George Ure   Tim Walton   Gary Wood

MITCHELL MAHONY
(Swing)

Training: Diane Blass School of Dance, and Queensland University of Technology, completing his Associate Degree in Dance. Other work includes: Royal Caribbean, Tokyo Disneyland and other commercial work. Mitchell is thrilled to be making his West End debut in *WICKED* and would love to thank his amazing friends and supportive family. For more information on Mitchell please visit www.reanimator.co.uk

RACHEL MULDOON
(Ensemble)

Training: Rachel trained with The Royal Ballet School & Laine Theatre Arts. Theatre includes: *Grease* (Piccadilly) - understudying/playing 'Marty' and 'Cha Cha'; Dance Captain for *The Genius of Ray Charles* (US tour); *Cinderella* (Wimbledon); *The Royal Variety Performance* 2005 (Millennium Centre); Dance Captain for *Abba Celebration* (Theatre Royal, Windsor); *So Shy* in *Aladdin* (Wimbledon); *A Royal Gala* (Millennium Centre); *The Royal Variety Performance* 2003 (Edinburgh Playhouse); *Beatrix Potter* (Royal Ballet Company). Television includes: *Children In Need; Passport to Paradise* (BBC); *Grease is the Word; Discomania 2; Madonnamania* (ITV1); *Milkshake Special* (Channel 5); *Ant and Dec's Saturday Night Takeaway* (LWT) and *Encounters* (Channel 4). Rachel would like to thank her family (especially her parents) for their love & support.

ADAM MURRAY
(Swing / Resident Dance Supervisor)

Training: Arts Educational School, London. Theatre includes: Assistant Choreographer to Bill Deamer on *The Ha'Penny Bridge* (Point, Dublin); *Seesaw* (ArtsEd); *We Will Rock You* (Dominion); Brian Conley's *Cinderella* (Mayflower, Southampton) and Dance Captain on *Encore Mr Producer!* (Jean Ann Ryan). TV includes: *Royal Variety Performance; Blue Peter; Children In Need;* dancer for *The Queen's Golden Jubilee Celebrations* and the BAFTA Awards (ITV) and dancer with Bruce Forsyth on his biographical documentary for ITV. Other work includes: soloist tap dancer to celebrate the work of Duke Ellington, conducted by Pete Long, and choreographic work for charity, fashion and trade shows, including Hugh Hefner's Cannes Film Festival celebration.

SEAN PARKINS
(Ensemble)

Training: Italia Conti Academy of Theatre Arts. Theatre includes: *On The Town* (ENO); *Dick Whittington* (Barbican); 'William' in *Mary Poppins* (Prince Edward Theatre); 'Tribe Member' in *Hair* (Gate Theatre); 'Mereb' in *Aida* (Germany); *Fame* (Aldwych); featured performer in Ann Reinking's *Broadway Theatre Project* and 'Tootles' in *Peter Pan* (Leicester Haymarket). Television includes: BBC's *Party in the Palace* (dir. by Trevor Nunn); *ZDF Wetten Das* (Germany); *Blue Peter; Disney Club; Nickelodeon* and Channel 4's *Buskers Odyssey.* Films include: *Harry Potter and the Philosopher's Stone.* Other work includes choreography for Kent Youth Ballet; Arts Centre Guildford; Italia Conti; Phil Collins' Little Dreams Foundation; Make A Wish Foundation; Big Foot Productions and Scream Company.

JAKE SAMUELS
(Ensemble, Fiyero u/s)

Training: Arts Educational School, Tring Park. Theatre includes: 'Brad Covitt' and 'Jim Upton' in Matthew Bourne's *Edward Scissorhands* (Sadler's Wells and International tour); 'Buddy' and 'Dexter Winthrop' in *Beautiful & Damned* (Lyric Theatre); 'Beast's Horse' in the RSC's *Beauty & the Beast* (Royal Shakespeare Theatre); 'Ruhrgold' and 'Nintendo' in *Starlight Express* (UK tour); 'Fred Casely' and 'Billy Flynn' in *Chicago* (UK tour, Japan and South Korea); ensemble, 'Vince Fontaine/Teen Angel' and 'Kenickie' in *Grease* (Dominion Theatre and UK tour). Films include: *Beyond the Sea.*

DAVID STOLLER
(Ensemble, Doctor Dillamond / Wizard u/s)

Training: David graduated from the University of Hertfordshire with a First Class BA (Hons) in Performing Arts and was awarded the Sir Nigel Hawthorne Award for Outstanding Achievement. Theatre includes: *Les Misérables* (Queens Theatre) understudying and playing 'Jean Valjean'; 'Elwood' in *The Official Tribute to the Blues Brothers* (European tour); 'The Specialist' in *Tommy* for Bill Kenwright (UK tour). Other work includes: television commercials for *Love It* magazine; Sun Bingo; Ford (Sky Sports); *The Richard and Judy Show* and a government Anti-Smoking campaign, a pilot for a new comedy sketch show, *When Mars Meets Venus* and a short film, *Shakespeare's Lost Pages.* This will be David's second year in *WICKED* and he wishes to thank his wife and two children for their constant support.

LIAM TAMNE
(Ensemble, Fiyero u/s)

Training: Laine Theatre Arts. Theatre includes: understudy 'Dandini' & 'Buttons' in *Cinderella* & understudy 'Prince' in *Snow White* (Manchester Opera House); lead singer & dancer at Oakwood Theme Park (Pembrokeshire); featured vocalist in *Believe In Yourself* & *Seeing Tomorrow* (Epsom Playhouse Theatre); 'Reynard the Fox' in *Mother Goose; Aladdin;* 'Cat' in *Dick Whittington* and 'Rolly' in *101 Dalmatians* (Belgrade Theatre, Coventry) and *An Evening with Val Doonican* (London Palladium Theatre). Television includes: *Songs of Praise Christmas Special* with Pete Waterman (BBC) and a documentary drama for the History Channel. Other work includes: modelling for *The Clothes Show Live* (NEC, Birmingham); Toni & Guy and Garb Fashion Shows.

CHLOE TAYLOR
(Swing)

Training: After 2 seasons with the National Youth Theatre, Chloe went on to train at the Arts Educational School, London. Theatre includes: 'Donna Marie' and 'Mrs Lyons' in *Blood Brothers* (Phoenix Theatre and national tour); 'Ada Figgins' in *Hobson's Choice* (Liverpool Neptune Theatre); *West Side Story in Concert* (Royal Albert Hall); 'Veronica' in Anthony Minghella's *Whale Music* (Medina Theatre, Isle of Wight); 'Belle' in *A Christmas Carol* (Liverpool Playhouse); *Whistle Down the Wind* (Southport Theatre) and 'Miss Syster' in a workshop of *The Ghost of Mrs Muir,* directed by Hugh Wooldridge. Other work includes: soloist on *Children In Need* (BBC Radio) and a recording of a Christmas album with Jimmy Cricket. Chloe is over the moon to be joining the cast of *WICKED* and would like to thank friends, Mum, Dad and Ged for their love and words of wisdom.

LINDSAY TAYLOR
(Ensemble)

Training: Little Theatre; Singers On Stage; Marymount, Manhattan College, BFA degree in Dance with honours, under the direction of Katie Langan Santee. Theatre includes: ensemble in *WICKED* (Apollo Victoria Theatre); featured actor and dancer in *So You Want To Be On Broadway* (Lambs Theatre); featured dancer and ensemble in *MMC Dance Company* (guest choreographers: Donald Byrd – *Drastic Cuts,* Sean Curren – *Curren Affair,* Joao Carovallo - *Karada,* Jamie Bishton - *Bend Towards Heaven,* Charlotte Griffen - *Coalescence);* featured singer in *American Entertainment* (Rye Playland). Teaching: Little Theatre, Littleton Colorado, USA.

EMILY TIERNEY
(Ensemble, Nessarose u/s)

Training: Emily graduated this April from Mountview Academy of Theatre Arts and is delighted to be making her West End debut in *WICKED.* Whilst training, roles included 'Alice Beane' in *Titanic - the Musical;* 'Johanna' in *Sweeney Todd;* 'Flaemchenn' in *Grand Hotel – the Musical;* 'Lady Ann' in *Richard III* and 'Phyll' in *Cider With Rosie* (Tour). Theatre: Emily made her professional debut earlier this year singing 'Maria' in *West Side Story* (Suite no.2) at the Barbican. Television: Emily can currently be seen playing the role of 'Alice' in the hit internet soap *Kate Modern.* Emily would like to thank the Tierney 'Von Traps' for EVERYTHING

HANNAH TOY
(Ensemble)

Training: Stage Door School of Dancing in Bournemouth under the tuition of Maureen and Julie Headford, and London Studio Centre. Theatre includes: *Dance Overture* at the Hackney Empire and New Wimbledon Theatre; principal solo dancer in *The Jazz Dance Company Tour* ending at the Peacock Theatre, London, directed by Petra Siniawski, choreographed by Dollie Henry, Anthony van Laast, David Leighton and Paul Roberts; Dance Captain in *Peter Pan* at The Anvil, Basingstoke, understudying 'Peter Pan' and 'Nitwit'; *Journey of Jazz* at the Lillian Baylis Theatre, Sadlers Wells, directed and choreographed by Dollie Henry. Hannah is delighted to be staying for a second year in *WICKED* and would like to thank her Mum, Nana, Sam and Antony for all their love and support.

GEORGE URE
(Ensemble, Boq u/s)

Training: George was born in Glasgow and has recently graduated from Mountview Academy of Theatre Arts. Roles whilst in training include 'Bride' in *Titanic;* 'Anthony' in *Sweeney Todd;* 'Chauffeur' in *Grand Hotel* and 'Macbeth' in *Macbeth.* Other work includes: series finalist in *Britannia High* for ITV Productions, which will be screened in the summer. George is thrilled to be making his West End debut in *WICKED* and would like to thank his Mum and amazing friends for all of their love and support. He would like to dedicate his performance to his Dad.

TIM WALTON
(Swing, Doctor Dillamond u/s)

Training: Diploma in Musical Theatre at Pretoria Technikon Dance Department, South Africa. Theatre includes: original London casts of *Mamma Mia!; The Witches of Eastwick; Romeo and Juliet; Tonight's The Night* and *WICKED.* West End: *The Woman In White; South Pacific* and *Starlight Express.* Regional: *Evita; The King and I; West Side Story; Hollywood Pinafore; Frogs; Fifty Million Frenchmen; The Mikado; HMS Pinafore* and *The Parson's Pirates.* Television includes: *Kidnapped Abroad* for Channel 5. Other work includes: Direction/Choreography of the South African première of *Ragtime* for Tshwane University of Technology.

GARY WOOD
(Swing)

Training: Performers College. Theatre includes: 'Richie' in *A Chorus Line* (Towngate Theatre); *Songs For A New World* (Performers Studio Theatre); *Whore!* (Los Altos Park) and *Rocking In To Christmas* (Ryde Theatre). Other work includes: 'The Candy Ball' (Grosvenor House Hotel); 'The Daisy Ball' (Grosvenor House Hotel) and the World Travel Market opening (London Excel).

hairspray

STARRING
MICHAEL BALL

'THE ULTIMATE FEEL-GOOD SHOW'

GUARDIAN

'A SUGAR RUSH OF PLEASURE'

DAILY TELEGRAPH

020 7379 5399 · SHAFTESBURY THEATRE · www.hairspraythemusical.co.uk

Above: Kerry Ellis • Top Left: Desmond Barrit • Top Right: Harriet Thorpe

Producers

MARC PLATT
Producer

Marc is represented on Broadway, in London, Melbourne, and throughout North America by *WICKED*. He also produced the Broadway debut of Richard Greenberg's play *Three Days of Rain,* starring Julia Roberts, directed by Joe Mantello; *Pal Joey* starring Christian Hoff and Stockard Channing and Matthew Bourne's ballet *Edward Scissorhands.* Films: *Rachel Getting Married,* directed by Jonathan Demme, starring Anne Hathaway and Debra Winger; *Wanted* starring Angelina Jolie, James McAvoy and Morgan Freeman; *Legally Blonde; Legally Blonde 2; Honey; Josie and the Pussycats; The Perfect Man; The Seeker.* Upcoming films: *Scott Pilgrim vs. The World,* directed by Edgar Wright, starring Michael Cera and *Nine* directed by Rob Marshall, starring Daniel Day-Lewis, Judi Dench, Nicole Kidman, Marion Cotillard, Penelope Cruz, Sophia Loren, Kate Hudson and Fergie. Television: HBO's *Empire Falls* (Golden Globe Award); *Once Upon A Mattress* (ABC); *The Path To 9/11* (ABC). Mr. Platt has served as president for three movie studios (Orion, TriStar and Universal).

UNIVERSAL PICTURES
Producer

Universal Pictures is a world leader in the production, marketing and distribution of motion pictures, including such franchise series as *The Mummy; American Pie; The Fast and the Furious; Meet the Parents; The Bourne Identity;* the Oscar® winners *Gladiator; Erin Brockovich; A Beautiful Mind; Ray* and *King Kong;* and the global sensation *Mamma Mia! The Movie.* Universal's upcoming films include *Duplicity,* starring Julia Roberts and Clive Owen; *Land of the Lost,* starring Will Ferrell; and *Public Enemies,* directed by Michael Mann and starring Johnny Depp and Christian Bale.

DAVID STONE
Producer

David Stone is currently represented around the world by *WICKED*. He has produced *The 25th Annual Putnam County Spelling Bee; Three Days of Rain; Man of La Mancha; The Vagina Monologues; Fully Committed; Lifegame; The Diary of Anne Frank; Full Gallop; The Santaland Diaries* and *Family Secrets.* David serves on the boards of The Broadway League and Broadway Cares/Equity Fights Aids. He also serves on the advisory boards of V-Day and Second Stage Theatre. David has lectured on theatre at the Juilliard School, NYU, Yale, Columbia and his alma mater, The University of Pennsylvania.

THE ARACA GROUP
Producer

Founded in 1997 by partners Matthew Rego, Michael Rego and Hank Unger, The Araca Group is a theatrical production and merchandise company. Araca's current and upcoming production credits include: eight productions of *Wicked* including Broadway and around the world; *Hairspray* (West End); and *Boeing-Boeing* (Broadway). Past Broadway and off-Broadway productions include: *Urinetown; The Wedding Singer; 'night, Mother; The Good Body; Frankie and Johnny in the Clair de Lune; Match; The Scene; Debbie Does Dallas; The Vagina Monologues; The Laramie Project;* and *Skyscraper.* In addition, The Araca Group develops and manages merchandise operations for *WICKED* (worldwide); *Jersey Boys* (London and Las Vegas); *The 25th Annual Putnam County Spelling Bee; The Wedding Singer; Hairspray* (West End); *Passing Strange;* Lincoln Center and Ivan Kane's Forty Deuce (Las Vegas).

JON B. PLATT
Producer

Mr. Platt is the three-time Tony Award-winning producer of *Copenhagen; Angels in America: Millennium Approaches* (Pulitzer Prize for Drama); and *Perestroika.* He is currently represented in New York, Chicago, Los Angeles, London, Tokyo, Melbourne and throughout North America by *WICKED*. This season Mr. Platt produced *Cyrano de Bergerac* on Broadway starring Kevin Kline and Jennifer Garner. He has received Tony Award nominations for his productions of *Damn Yankees; Peter Pan; Hello, Dolly!; The Diary of Anne Frank; Lonesome West; Man of La Mancha* and *WICKED.* Mr. Platt has produced numerous national tours including: *The Sound of Music; Sunset Boulevard; Hair; Jesus Christ Superstar; Fiddler on the Roof; The Best Little Whorehouse in Texas; A Chorus Line; The Graduate;* and *Blue Man Group "Tubes".* Mr. Platt is represented in New York by the off Broadway smash hit *Forbidden Broadway: Rude Awakening,* celebrating its 26th year.

MICHAEL McCABE
UK Executive Producer

As well as being Executive Producer of the London production, Michael is also a consultant for *WICKED* at the Palladium Theater in Stuttgart. He was the International Marketing Director (and subsequently also the Associate Producer) of Benny Andersson and Björn Ulvaeus' smash hit musical *Mamma Mia!,* from 1998-2004. He devised and implemented the marketing strategy for the London premiere production and for numerous productions around the world, including Broadway, Las Vegas and Toronto. Michael was Associate Producer, with CMP, of *Swimming with Sharks* starring Christian Slater at the Vaudeville Theatre. As an independent marketing advisor and consultant, Michael has worked with companies including Cirque du Soleil, English National Opera, Stage Entertainment and for Disney Theatrical Productions in London, Hamburg, Amsterdam and Paris.
www.michaelmccabeproductions.com

Above: Dianne Pilkington • Top Left: Andy Mace • Top Right: Oliver Tompsett and Dianne Pilkington

Park Plaza Victoria
LONDON
Official Hotel Partner - www.ParkPlaza.com

iVillage.co.uk
Visit the official UK fan forum at
www.ivillage.co.uk/wicked

Original Broadway Cast Recording on
DECCA BROADWAY

Wicked: The Life & Times of the Wicked Witch of the West
by Gregory Maguire is published in the UK by:
headline review
www.readingcircle.co.uk

victoria Partnership Limited
www.victoria-partnership.co.uk

South Westminster Renewal Partnership
www.southwestminster.org.uk

THE *Make-Up Brush* COMPANY

M·A·C

WICKED is proud to support:

Bliss
for babies born too soon,
too small, too sick
www.bliss.org.uk

[anti bullying alliance]
www.anti-bullyingalliance.org.uk

Thrive
using gardening to change lives
www.thrive.org.uk

the abbey centre
www.theabbeycentre.org.uk

PRODUCTION CREDITS

FOR WICKED LONDON

General Management	Nick Salmon & Nia Janis
	Act Productions
Production Manager	Richard Bullimore
Assistant Production Manager	Timandra Dyer
Costume Supervisor	Margie Bailey
Deputy Costume Supervisor	Sandy Smith Wilson
UK Lighting Associate	Michael Odam
Wigs Supervisor	J. Jared Janas
Props Supervisor	Jane Slattery
Master Carpenter	Stephen Herbert
Deputy Master Carpenter	Stu Holden
Chargehand Stage Technician/	
Head Flyman	Wayne Pottinger
Chargehand	Stuart Taylor
Stage Crew	Brendan Archer
	Nic Cater
	Robert Dunlop
	Richard Green
	Ben Haslam
	Sosthenes Marques
	Mark McGurran
	Jamie Paterson
	Marcus Reddington
	Nigel Shephard
Head of Automation	Adam Harvey
Deputy Automation	Peter Wakeman
Assistant Automation	Adam Calver
Wardrobe Manager	Jonathan Skinner
Deputy Wardrobe Manager	Jen Goodwin
Wardrobe Assistant	Caroline Findlay
Wardrobe Assistant	Sophie Blenkinsop
Dressers	Ali Bell, Theresa Burke, Paula Eastman, Naimen Ebdon, Davina Elliott, Holly Ellis, Lizzie Furniss, Hannah Grammel, Joanna Hunt, Andrew Keelan, Jeff Krowell, Jacqueline Richardson, Evelina Salvi, Sarah Small, Naomi Taylor, Joanna Thompson, Lydia Young
Chief Electrician	Damian Ridge
Deputy Chief Electrician	Dominic Airs
Chargehand LX	Hazel Paterson
Followspots / Stage Electricians	Emily Canetta
	James Couper
	Alex Howard
	Matt Sherrin
	Lara Sims
	Berni Wallace
	Matt Walford
Head of Sound	Hyder "H" Khalil
Deputy Sound	Julie Cole
Assistant Sound	Janee Robinson
Head of Hair and Make-Up	Jo Nielson
Deputy Wigs and Make-Up	Vanya Pell
Wigs Assistant	Kate Griffiths
Wigs Assistant	Lucy Hunter
Wigs Assistant	Holly Silius
Wigs Assistant	Natalie Smith
Wigs Assistant	Georgia Woodland
Synthesizer Programming	Phij Adams

LONDON PRODUCTION CREDITS

Senior Production Carpenter	Dominic Addy
Production Carpenters	Nick Smith
	Micky Fernandez
	Dave Simmons
Senior Rigger	Simon Stone
Riggers	Kevin Carro
	Howard Woodliffe
	Mark Davis
	Chris Evans
	Jody Keys
Senior Production Automation Engineer	Mike Sharp
Production Automation Engineer	Ben Pickersgill
Production Automation	Pete Quinlan
	Simon Roberts
	Luke Skoug
Costume Head Buyer	Caroline Waterman
Costume Administrator	Christine Toal
Costume Accessories	Rebecca Elson
Costume Assistant Shoes	Elizabeth Perridge
Costume Assistants	Louise Cassettari, Claire Collins, Jess Glover, Melanie Larkin
Senior Production Electrician	Peter Lambert
Production Electricians	Chris Luscombe
	Mike Dixon
	Stephen Reeve
	Stuart Porter
	Sara Lunn
	Alistair Grant
Conventional Programmers	Pryderi Baskerville
	Philipp-S. Herbst
	Johannes Gruber
Senior Production Sound Engineer	Ken Hampton
Production Sound Engineers	Tim Stephens
	Steve Owen
	Greg Pink
	Andy Jackson
	Tim Rawlings
	Dan Gregory
Set Built and Painted by	TMS International
Draperies by	Ken Creasey
Set Engineering by	Delstar Engineering
Specialist Set Electrics by	Howard Eaton Lighting
Automation by	Stage Technologies
Costumes made by	Martin Adams, Angels, Amanda Barrow, Jackie Burston, Mr D Bruno, Karen Crichton, Mark Costello, Sally Ann Dicksee, Amanda Haslam, Naomi Isaacs, Sascha Kier, Dawn Korner, Caroline Lanyon, Christine Manning, Paul Manning, Kevin Mathias, Phil Reynolds, Lorraine Richards, Karen Sharp, Carole Thompson, Celia Pierce, Mervyn Wallace
Hats by	Sean Barrett, Simon Dawes, Karen Shannon
Undergarments provided by	Bra*Tenders, New York
Embroidery by	Clifton Canvas, Hand and Lock, Jen Goodwin, Lorna Nathan, Mrudula Patel, Daphne Randall, Steve Williams
Gloves by	Cornelia James, Pamela Woods
Jewellery by	Martin Adams
Knitting by	Trevor Collins
Fabric Printing by	Hatley Prints
Fabric Effects	Gabrielle Firth, Penny Hadrill, Hatley Prints, Nicola Kileen, Gilli Thompson
Prosthetics and Wings by	Robert Allsop
Shoe Makers	Gamba Theatricals Ltd, K&D Shoes, La Duca
Lighting Supplied by	PRG Europe
Sound Supplied by	Autograph Sound Recording
Projection Equipment Supplied by	Creative Technology
Flying Effects Advisor	Freedom Flying
Prop Costumes by	Robert Allsop, Applied Arts, Ben Brown, Jeannie Fletcher

Furniture & Props by	Heron & Driver
	Artisan 2003 Ltd
	Calmel Design & Construction
	Russell Craig
	Helen Pettitt
	Russell Beck Studio
	Greenprops
	John Creech Design
	Den Design Studio
Nessarose Furniture Painted by	Belinda Clisham
Prop Transport by	Props Mobile
Puppets	Bob Flanagan
Rigging supplied by	Unusual Rigging
Electrical Contractors	RWS Electrical & Audio Contractors
Rehearsal Set by	Andy Latham Scenery
Risk Assessor	Rodger Neate
Transport	GH Luckings & Sons
International Shipping	Jackie Jupp Project Management
Opening Night production & Logistics by	The Hospital Events Company - Michael Berg (020 7170 9100)
Production Lawyer	Neil Adleman at Harbottle & Lewis
Production Insurance by	Walton and Parkinson
Production Accountant	Neil Laidlaw at Act Productions
Production Photographer	Tristram Kenton
Merchandise	The Araca Group
Press and PR	Public Eye (020 7351 1555)
Advertising, Marketing and Graphics	Dewynters (020 7321 0488)
Broadcast & Digital Media	MediaCom (020 7158 5500)
Digital Design & Marketing	Gavin Nugent for UVFX www.uvfx.tv
Sales & Marketing Consultant	Martin Barrow for Martin Barrow Limited (020 7404 3212)
Educational Materials created by	Kids Connections www.KidsConnections.co.uk

PRODUCTION ACKNOWLEDGEMENTS

Fight Director	Terry King
Casting Co-ordinator	Natalie Gallagher
Assistant Casting Director	James Hopson
Rehearsal studio	Duthy Hall
Apartments provided by	Nora Guhnfeldt of Citylife Apartments
Travel Agent	Chris Mack for GE Travel

FOR WICKED WORLDWIDE

General Management	Nina Essman, Nancy Gibbs and Marcia Goldberg for 321 Theatrical Management
US Company Manager	Susan Sampliner
Production Supervisor	Thom Widmann
Production Administrator	Robert Brinkerhoff
Assistant Director	Paul Dobie
Dance Supervisors	Corinne McFadden-Herrera, Patrick McCollum
Assistant to Mr Schwartz	Michael Cole
Assistant Scenic Designers	Nick Francone, Jonathan Spencer
Oz Map Design	Francis Keeping
Associate Costume Designers	Michael Sharpe, Amanda Whidden
Associate Lighting Designer	Karen Spahn
Associate Lighting Designer / Moving Lights	Warren Flynn
Projection Programmer	Hillary Knox
Assistant to Projection Designer	Anne E. McMills
Projection Animators	Gareth Smith, Ari Sachter Zeltzer
Associate Sound Designer	Kai Harada
Assistant to Wig & Hair Designer	Alfonso Annotto
Makeup Design	Joe Dulude II
Production Carpenter	Rick Howard
Production Props	George Wagner
Production Wardrobe Supervisor	Alyce Gilbert
Music Preparation	Anixter Rice Music Services
Synthesizer Programming	Andrew Barrett for Lionella Productions, Ltd.
Accountant	Robert Fried, C.P.A.
Legal Counsel	Loeb and Loeb, Seth Gelblum
Legal Counsel for Universal Pictures	Keith Blau

FOR MARC PLATT PRODUCTIONS

Adam Siegel, Greg Lessans, Joey Levy,
Jared LeBoff, Nik Mavinkurve, Tia Maggini,
Dana Krupinski, Adam Wilkins, Conor Welch

FOR STONE PRODUCTIONS

Producing Associate	Patrick Catullo
Executive Assistant	Aaron Glick

UNIVERSAL PICTURES

President & COO, Universal Studios, Inc.	Ron Meyer
Chairman	Marc Shmuger
Co-Chairman	David Linde
President of Marketing & Distribution	Adam Fogelson
President of Marketing	Eddie Egan
Co-President, Production & EVP, Universal Pictures	Jimmy Horowitz

FOR MICHAEL McCABE PRODUCTIONS

Producer	Michael McCabe
Production Associate	Luke Shires
Legal	Neil Adleman at Harbottle & Lewis
Accountants	Collins & Company

ACT PRODUCTIONS LTD

Chairman	Roger Wingate
Director of Production	Nick Salmon
Producer	Matthew Byam Shaw
General Manager	Nia Janis
Production Administrator	Janet Powell
Production Assistant	Amardeep Kamboz
Production Assistant	Georgia Gatti
Production Assistant	Bailey Lock
Administrative Assistant	Charlotte Sutton
Head of Finance	Kerrie Cronin
Production Accountant	Kate Barraball
Payroll Manager	Anna Collins
Accounts Assistant	Tiffany Harold
Associate Producer	Roger Chapman

Act Productions Intern funded by The Stage One Producer Placement Scheme
(www.stageone.uk.com for more information.)

THANKS TO

Arturo Barquet; Jake Bell; David Blandon; Craig Burns; Tim Carlton-Jones; Jo Danvers; Hollace Davids; Lucy Evans; Patrick Gracey; Highly Sprung; Suzie Hills; David Kosse; John Lewis Partnership; Jo Luke; New Heights; Kristen Oei; Linda Pace-Alexander; Sarah Preece; Jonathan Rutter; Serino Coyne Inc.; Chic Silber; Allyson Simpson; Cathy Small; Kat Smiley; Neils Swinkels; and Bernard Telsey.

In loving memory of Bob Fennell, Ruth Rosenberg and Karen Shaw

WICKED UK Graphics ©WLPL. Graphics adapted by Dewynters, London based on an original concept by Serino Coyne Inc., New York.

Oliver Tompsett

the
Apollo Victori

Photograph by David Thrower, Redshift Photography with Hoare Lea Lighting

The Shows

Theatre History

Opened as a cinema in 1930 the now "Apollo Victoria" is a 2348 capacity theatrical venue brimming with art deco design. In the era where talking pictures were influencing the creation of "super" cinemas, Provincial Cinematograph Theatres (PCT) invited Ernest Walmsley Lewis to submit plans to build such a cinema a stone's throw away from Victoria Station. It was one of Britain's first cinemas to be listed for its architectural significance and is now a Grade 2 listed building.

Designing the venue was challenging to say the least especially due to the disadvantage of having two major roads running either side of it. Having two frontages were considered very severe; taxi drivers were said to have nicknamed the venue "Sing-Sing".

The interior was inspired, unique and a testament to art deco design. "Imagine a fairy cavern under the sea, or a mermaid's dream of heaven; something one has never seen or thought of before; huge submarine flowers against the walls that branch up and out and throw mysterious light towards the realms above, and glassy illuminated stalactites hanging from the ceiling; and a proscenium like a slender host of silver trees, and silvered organ pipes that shoot up to the roof; while over the whole the lights change from deep-sea green to the colours of the dawn, and from these to the warm comfort sunlight" – Gaumont-British News. On 15th October 1930, the New Victoria opened with the film *Old English* and a stage show called *Hoop-La.* Years of highs and lows followed. Now heading into its 76th year the Cinema has transformed into one of the leading West End venues hosting musicals such as *The Sound of Music* with Petula Clark, *Camelot* with Richard Harris, and *Fiddler on the Roof* with Topol.

In 1984 The Apollo Victoria became host to Andrew Lloyd Webber's super charged *Starlight Express*, with special building consent granted to allow the set to be built into the main auditorium to allow the skaters access at all levels linked by a 5-tonne revolving bridge. After 18 very successful years, *Starlight Express* had its final performance at this theatre on 12th January 2002.

Since this time the Apollo Victoria has undergone major restoration works and all features previously hidden by the vast *Starlight Express* set have now been restored to their former glory and are once again visible to our patrons. The theatre is now one of the finest in London.

Bombay Dreams started previewing from 31st May 2002, and had its opening night on 19th June 2002. After over two extremely successful years, *Bombay Dreams* left for America in June 2004. Three weeks later the legend that is *Saturday Night Fever* moved in, lighting up the West End in a disco extravaganza, taking us back to the 70s. The show opened on 2nd July 2004 and was a huge success having the audience dancing in the aisles until it closed on 18th February 2006.

On 28th March, 2006 Billy Joel's smash hit Broadway show *Movin' Out* opened for an 8 week run at the Apollo Victoria. Fans of the show and Billy Joel from all over the world came to see the amazing rock ballet choreographed by the renowned Twyla Tharp.

The Apollo Victoria Theatre has seen more changes over the last year with restoration work taking it back to its original glory. It wasn't long before the lights were shining and seats were full, ready for the amazing opening of the long awaited smash hit musical *WICKED* but its unique style and stature are sure to remain.

a Theatre

The theatre that became the Emerald City

The Apollo Victoria (the New Victoria) is one of the most exciting cine-theatres ever built in Britain. It opened with films and stage shows, but it could almost have been designed with the present show in mind. It is a magical gateway to the Emerald City of the Wizard of Oz.

The architect, a young man named Ernest Wamsley Lewis, working with Gaumont's W E Trent, produced a design of striking originality. It was like no other. The foyer was a riot of colourful Art Deco, while the auditorium was a dreamlike place of submarine forms and changing lights, 'a mermaid's palace' (as Lewis described it) at the bottom of the ocean. A wave-pattern carpet on the stairs carried the visitor from the brilliant foyer to this mysterious world below.

Just a year before *WICKED* opened these wonderful designs had been almost obliterated. The foyer and staircase walls had been painted over with a depressing maroon coating and many other decorative features and finishes had been completely lost. But in 2006 Live Nation set about a restoration project which, even in its first few months, had achieved spectacular results.

The iron railings on the staircase are now again emerald green. The black and silver-channelled foyer walls have been restored and the ceiling, with its crisp prismatic ornaments is, once more, seen in dazzling silver. The stairs have regained their wavy carpet and their delicately inlaid grey sycamore linings (actually a feat of graining by the most accomplished craftspeople in the business) while seaweeds and fishes again decorate the landing walls.

The auditorium has had much of its wonderful sense of mystery restored. The restored shell uplighters fill the space with a green glow, changing softly to blue and amber, then back to green, giving the impression of light filtered through to the ocean depths. The voyage to the Emerald City now seems complete.

The restoration project still has a little way to go. Work has to be fitted into the brief gaps that occur in the crowded programme of a major music house, but what has already been done amounts to a brilliant achievement.

Research by the architect and conservation experts uncovered some historical puzzles. The road frontages were intended by Lewis to be the first London example of what German cinema designers of the 1930s called 'light architecture', but his original intention, to accentuate the horizontal lines of the facades with thin neon strips, proved technically unachievable. Modern technology has made it possible to do what he could not do. The pencil-thin green lines that now light the facades produce the exact effect he intended - and in a colour that the producers of *WICKED* might have chosen themselves.

One mystifying aspect of the 1930 design can be seen on the first half landing, viewed from the foyer. Here there is a lovely low-relief figure of 'The Spirit of the Film', the work of sculptor Newbury A Trent. As completed, this was a stylised, completely nude female figure, surrounded by swirling strips of film. But now she wears flimsy, transparent drapes! There is no record of why or when these garments were applied.

The quality of the modelling makes it almost certain that the original artist was responsible and the alteration probably occurred very early in the life of the theatre. Whatever caused the change, this beautiful relief, stripped of insensitive overpainting, is now seen in its original deep green colour for the first time in decades.

The conservation and continuing decorative restoration of this extraordinary theatre is a great credit to the building owners. They have called on the skills of many experts, but the most significant aspect of the project has been the spirit of cooperation between the architectural team and the officials of English Heritage and Westminster City Council who exercise listed building controls. Live Nation is actively showing its commitment to custodianship of a twentieth century building of outstanding national importance, while the officials recognise that the best way of ensuring the preservation of the theatre is to keep it in full use as a home for big audience events. It is a striking demonstration of the way in which London's wonderful Theatreland can be enriched and secured for the future.

For Live Nation Venues

President - Paul Latham
Financial Director - Stuart Douglas
Divisional Manager (South) - Stephen Murtagh

For the Apollo Victoria Theatre

General Manager – Ben Phillips
Deputy General Manager – Anita Daniel
Assistant Theatre Manager - Rob Noverraz
Chief Electrician - Oliver Baldock
Stage Manager – Jon Arden
Box Office Manager - Peter Flanagan
Front of House Manager- Annette Hannigan

Terms And Conditions Of Sale

Admission: For performances, the Apollo Victoria Theatre opens 1 hour before performance time. Latecomers may not be admitted until a suitable break in the performance and, in some instances, not until the interval. The management reserves the right to refuse admission. We would ask you to respect performers and patrons by avoiding undue noise and disruption.

Babes in arms are not permitted into the venue. We advise parents that the performance is not suitable for children under 8, although this is at the parents' discretion. All children must have a ticket and booster cushions are available.

Once purchased, tickets cannot be refunded or exchanged.

Photography and recording of events are strictly prohibited.

Guests are reminded to keep personal belongings with them at all times whilst in the theatre. When leaving the theatre please also be aware that pickpockets may operate in this area.

All alcoholic and soft drinks may be taken into the auditorium as long as they are in a plastic cup available from any of our bars. The Apollo Victoria is a strictly NO smoking venue, patrons are kindly asked to smoke outside the venue.

The safety curtain will be lowered and raised in the presence of each audience.

Theatre Rules And Regulations

In accordance with the requirements of The City of Westminster the following conditions must be observed

1. The public may leave at the end of the performance by all exit doors and such doors must at all times be open.

2. All gangways, staircases and passageways shall be entirely free from chairs and any other obstructions.

3. Persons shall not be permitted to stand or sit in any of the gangways. If standing is permitted in the gangways at the sides and rear of the seating it shall be strictly limited to the numbers indicated in the notices exhibited in those areas.

4. The management reserve the right to change this programme without notice and are not held responsible for the non appearance of any artist.

5. The management reserves the right to refuse admittance. The use of cameras and recording equipment of any kind are strictly forbidden in the auditorium.

6. Please switch off all mobile phones and pagers before entering the auditorium.

Facilities

Special access requirements: there are 4 wheelchair spaces available for each performance. Please call 0207 828 7074 to book and for further details. Tickets are to be booked in advance and seating for an escort will be provided in a nearby seat.

Bars and interval drinks: the Apollo Victoria Theatre has 4 bars situated in the main foyer, dress circle foyer and the rear of the stalls. We strongly advise that you place interval orders at any of these bars to avoid queuing during the interval.

Kiosks and confectionary: there are 2 main kiosks within the theatre situated in the main foyer, selling a variety of sweets, ice creams and drinks. A small selection of confectionary can also be found at each bar.

Advance orders: parties are able to organise special hospitality packages to their needs, whether for an anniversary or large party please call 020 7592 1381.

Hearing Loop: the theatre auditorium is equipped with a loop system for hearing impaired patrons. To hire a headset please ask at the cloakroom just off the main foyer. A refundable deposit of £10 is required.

Lost Property: if you have lost any items during your visit please telephone 0207 834 6318 between 10.30am and 5.00pm Monday-Friday.

Published by The Araca Group
Photography by Tristram Kenton
This edition published December 2008

Special Thanks: Michael McCabe, Patrick Catullo, Jo Danvers, Dewynters, Patrick Gracey, Nia Janis, Deborah Koo, Erin Krass, Joey Levy, Marc Platt, Nick Salmon, Susan Sampliner, David Stone and Mark Taylor.

For additional copies and other WICKED merchandise, visit www.WickedTheMusical.co.uk or contact: The Araca Group: 545 West 45 Street 10th Floor New York, NY 10036
001 212-869-0070

The information contained within is correct at the time of publication. All materials used by permission. All rights reserved. No part of this book may be used or reproduced in any manner whatsoever without the written permission of the publisher. Copyright The Araca Group, LLC 2008.

Above: 2008/09 Company • Top Left: Jeremy Legat • Top Right: Caroline Keiff

Harriet Thorpe

Desmond Barrit

Original London Company